THE PLAN

How God got the
world ready for JESUS

Sinclair B. Ferguson

Illustrated by Angelo Ruta

A gift given with love to

....

....

....

from

....

....

....

Psalm 40:5

Are you ready? Ready for what?
Are you ready for a birthday, for
school, for Christmas? If you want to be ready you
have to be organised. And if you want to be organised you
need a really good plan.

Take Christmas for example. There are presents to buy
and cards to send. You will have to go shopping. Make sure
you buy enough stamps for the Christmas cards! There are
also special meals to cook.

Sometimes family members and other visitors will come
to see you. Lots of things happen at Christmas time. That is
why you need to get organised and make a list of the things
you want to do. You need a good plan!

God also made a plan for the very first Christmas. It was
an important plan. It was a master plan. In fact it was a perfect
plan!

First of all, God needed to get different people from several places to go to the same place. Some had to come from very far away. Others just had to travel a short distance.

But where did they have to go?

They had to travel to a little village in the middle of nowhere called Bethlehem.

Who were these people?

Well, there was Mary and Joseph, several wise men, some shepherds and a great crowd of angels. But who was the most important person to come to Bethlehem?

Yes! It was the baby Jesus. God had promised that his Son, the Saviour, would be born in Bethlehem.

However, before that could happen God had to get Mary and Joseph to leave their hometown of Nazareth.

He also had to get the shepherds to leave their flocks in the middle of the night and get the wise men to travel many, many miles from the east.

But who had to travel the farthest to get to Bethlehem? That's right – Jesus. God sent his Son, the Lord Jesus, from heaven.

That's a lot of things to organise! How did God do it? The first part of the plan was to get the wise men to leave their homes. It would be a long journey so they had to set off before anyone else. God knew that they would need help so the first thing he gave them was a star.

Why did they need that? Well these wise men spent a lot of time looking at the stars. They thought the way the stars were arranged in the night sky could tell them what was going to happen on Earth. So God gave them a star they had never seen before. It shone very brightly in the sky.

When they saw it they said, 'Look at that star shining brightly in the sky! What does it mean?'

They searched their old books to find the answer.

The star seemed to keep moving. 'We have never seen that star before. It must mean that the great new king has been born.' They were very excited. 'Let's get ready to follow it,' they said.

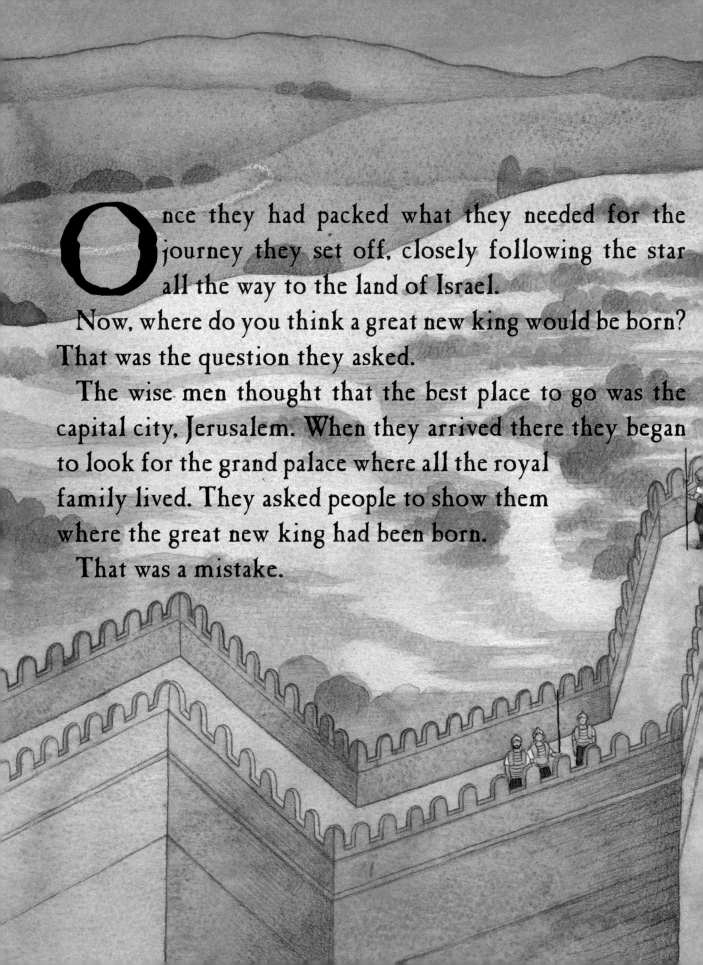

Once they had packed what they needed for the journey they set off, closely following the star all the way to the land of Israel.

Now, where do you think a great new king would be born? That was the question they asked.

The wise men thought that the best place to go was the capital city, Jerusalem. When they arrived there they began to look for the grand palace where all the royal family lived. They asked people to show them where the great new king had been born.

That was a mistake.

King Herod heard of it and was very upset. He was the king! No babies had been born in the palace recently. Was someone plotting to get rid of him? What could all this mean? Herod decided to meet the wise men and listen to their story. Some of it sounded familiar. One of his advisers fetched the scroll of the Old Testament prophet Micah.

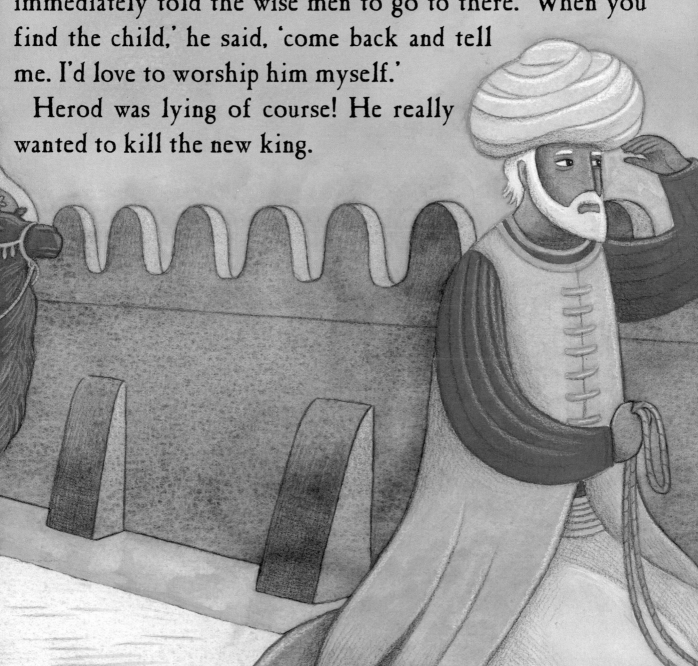

When the advisers looked up the scroll they read these words: 'From you Bethlehem, one will go forth from me to be ruler in Israel. He comes from long ago, from eternity.'

The new king would be born in Bethlehem! Herod immediately told the wise men to go to there. 'When you find the child,' he said, 'come back and tell me. I'd love to worship him myself.'

Herod was lying of course! He really wanted to kill the new king.

The wise men then left the city but this time they made sure that they followed the star carefully. Eventually they arrived at the place where the young child Jesus was.

Mary and Joseph were not in a royal palace. They were not rich people. The wise men must have thought, 'How can this baby be the great new king?'

But Jesus wasn't just a baby, he wasn't just an ordinary king either – he was the Son of God – the King of all kings.

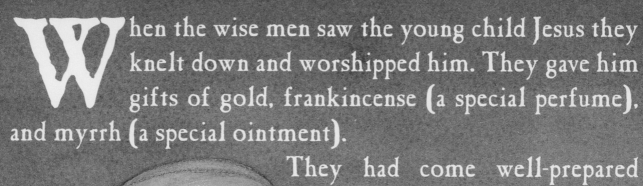

Wh:en the wise men saw the young child Jesus they knelt down and worshipped him. They gave him gifts of gold, frankincense (a special perfume), and myrrh (a special ointment).

They had come well-prepared for the first Christmas – even although they didn't know it was the first Christmas!

That night God warned the wise men in a dream not to return to King Herod because he wanted to harm Jesus. They quickly left the land of Israel by a different road and travelled the long hard journey home to the East.

It had all been a part of God's plan. He wanted people from far away to know about Jesus. He still does.

Now we mustn't forget the shepherds. They didn't need a star to guide them to Bethlehem because they lived in the hills just outside the village and knew exactly where Bethlehem was.

The problem with the shepherds was that they hardly ever left their sheep. They would need something very special to make them believe that God was telling them to leave their flocks and go and find a baby!

So God sent them an angel!

The shepherds were scared out of their wits. What was this? What was happening to them?

Then the angel spoke.

'Don't be afraid!' the angel announced. 'I have wonderful news for you. A Saviour has been born today. Go into Bethlehem, and you will find him. You will recognise the baby. He is lying in a manger and his mother has wrapped him up in cloths.'

Suddenly a whole crowd of angels appeared. The shepherds were taken by surprise, because all these angels were praising God. What a sound they made. 'Glory to God in the Highest!' they were saying.

'Peace on earth to those whom God shows his love and mercy!'

Now the shepherds knew that if the baby was lying in a manger he must be inside a stable. But babies aren't usually born in stables and mums and dads don't normally put their little children to sleep in mangers.

However, when Mary and Joseph had reached Bethlehem there was no room for them anywhere. The only shelter they could get was a stable and the only bed they could find for their newborn baby was a dirty old food trough.

When the shepherds saw the stable and the manger with the baby inside it, just as the angel had said, they knew that this baby really was the Son of God – he really was their Saviour.

That was why the shepherds went throughout the whole village telling everybody about what they had seen and heard. They had such good news to share. The Saviour of the world had been born.

But neither the wise men, nor the shepherds would have come into Bethlehem were it not for three other people.

Yes, God needed to get Mary and Joseph to Bethlehem. How did he do that?

art of God's plan was to use the Roman Emperor, Caesar Augustus. God arranged things so that Caesar needed to raise more taxes. Caesar decided to get all the people in Israel to return to the towns that they had been born in. He would then get officials to write down their names and where they lived so that he could collect the money later.

All the people whose families came from Bethlehem had to move back there to get counted. Caesar Augustus had no idea that he was part of God's master plan to send Mary and Joseph to Bethlehem. Isn't God amazing? Next, God had to get the baby Jesus there.

Part of God's plan for his Son was to give him a family to look after him and care for him – but also a family that would go way back into history. As well as Mary and Joseph there was Abraham and Isaac, Jacob and Judah.

However, God's Son needed something else. He needed a name. He was coming into the world to do one special thing. His name would tell people what he would do. So God told Mary and Joseph to call the baby 'Jesus' because he would save his people from their sins.

Right from the beginning God's plan was that Jesus would live a perfect life. Because Jesus had no sins this meant that he was the only one who could save his people from their sins. He was the only one who could take the punishment that sinners deserved.

That is why Jesus came. It was a brilliant plan. But it was also a dangerous one – for Jesus. For the next thirty three years he obeyed his Father perfectly. After Jesus died on the cross in our place his Father raised him from the dead. Later he went back to heaven to be with him. The Lord Jesus Christ is there today, loving us and watching over us.

One day Jesus will come back again. And then he will begin a new world. This is God's magnificent plan – the plan that began before time began – the plan for the very first Christmas.

So that is how God got ready for the first Christmas. God the Father sent his Son Jesus because he loves his people very much. God knew we could never take away our own sins. His Son, the Lord Jesus, was willing to do that for us.

Here is a verse from the Bible which tells us why God sent Jesus:

'God so loved the world that he gave his only Son that whoever (which includes you and me) believes in him will not perish but have everlasting life.' John 3:16.

I think that's absolutely wonderful, don't you?

Are you trusting in the Lord Jesus? Have you told him that you want to be his friend and follower all your life? You need to be ready to meet with God – and for that you'll need to have your sins forgiven. The only way to have your sins forgiven is to trust in the Lord Jesus Christ. If you want to be a friend of Jesus and to live for him here is a prayer to say:

Heavenly Father, I want to thank you for your marvellous Christmas plan. Thank you for bringing the Wise men and the Shepherds. You have shown us that Jesus wants to be the Saviour for ordinary and clever people as well as people from all over the world. Thank you for bringing Mary and Joseph who looked after the Lord Jesus when he was just a little baby.

Lord Jesus, thank you for being our Saviour and for dying on the cross to show us your love and to take away our sins. Thank you that you rose again. You are always with those who trust and love you.

Heavenly Father. We look forward so much to giving and receiving presents. Help us to open our hearts to the Lord Jesus. Help us to trust him as our Saviour and obey him as our Lord. Help us to give our lives to him as our gift to you. We pray these things in the name of your Son, the great new king, the Lord Jesus. Amen.

Christian Focus Publications publishes books for adults and children under its four main imprints: Christian Focus, Christian Heritage, CF4K and Mentor. Our books reflect that God's Word is reliable and Jesus is the way to know him, and live for ever with him.

Our children's publication list includes a Sunday School curriculum that covers pre-school to early teens and puzzle and activity books. We also publish personal and family devotional titles, biographies and inspirational stories that children will love.

If you are looking for quality Bible teaching for children then we have an excellent range of Bible stories and age specific theological books. From pre-school board books to teenage apologetics, we have it covered!

Find us at our web page: www.christianfocus.com

10 9 8 7 6 5 4 3 2
Copyright © Sinclair B Ferguson 2009
Christian Focus Publications
ISBN: 978-1-84550-451-9
Reprinted 2015
Published by Christian Focus Publications,
Geanies House, Fearn, Tain, Ross-shire,
IV20 1TW, Scotland, U.K.

Cover design by Daniel van Straaten
Illustrations by Angelo Ruta
Printed by Gutenberg Press in Malta

CF4•K
Because you're never too young to know Jesus